MW01153396

RECORD BREAKERS
SOCCER

www.av2books.com

MEDIA ENHANCED BOOKS
AV²
BY WEIGL
ADDED VALUE • AUDIO VISUAL

BOOK CODE

P462373

AV² by Weigl brings you media enhanced books that support active learning.

AV² provides enriched content that supplements and complements this book. Weigl's AV² books strive to create inspired learning and engage young minds for a total learning experience.

Go to **www.av2books.com**, and enter this book's unique code. You will have access to video, audio, web links, quizzes, a slide show, and activities.

Audio
Listen to sections of the book read aloud.

Video
Watch informative video clips.

Web Link
Find research sites and play interactive games.

Try This!
Complete activities and hands-on experiments.

Due to the dynamic nature of the Internet, some of the URLs and activities provided as part of AV² by Weigl may have changed or ceased to exist. AV² by Weigl accepts no responsibility for any such changes. All media enhanced books are regularly monitored to update addresses and sites in a timely manner. Contact AV² by Weigl at 1-866-649-3445 or av2books@weigl.com with any questions, comments, or feedback.

Published by AV² by Weigl
350 5th Avenue, 59th Floor
New York, NY 10118
Website: www.av2books.com   www.weigl.com

Library of Congress Cataloging-in-Publication Data

Wiseman, Blaine.
 Soccer / Blaine Wiseman.
   p. cm. -- (Record breakers)
 Includes index.
 ISBN 978-1-61690-106-6 (hardcover : alk. paper) -- ISBN 978-1-61690-107-3 (softcover : alk. paper) -- ISBN 978-1-61690-108-0 (e-book)
 1. Soccer--Records--Juvenile literature. I. Title.
 GV943.4.W58 2011
 796.334--dc22
                          2010006156

Printed in the United States of American in North Mankato, Minnesota
1 2 3 4 5 6 7 8 9 0 14 13 12 11 10

052010
WEP264000

Project Coordinator Heather C. Hudak
Design Terry Paulhus

Contents

The Players

Pelé is one of the best-known soccer players in history. Born Edson Arantes do Nascimento, he was given the nickname Pelé, which means "miracle" in **Hebrew**. People all over the world enjoyed watching Pelé play. In 1969, Pelé played a game in Nigeria, where a war was taking place. The two sides called a **cease-fire** so they could watch Pelé play. Pelé, who grew up shining shoes on the streets of Brazil, holds several world soccer records.

Most professional goals – 1,281
Pelé scored his first professional goal when he was only 16 years old.

Most World Cup championships – 3
Pelé won the World Cup in 1958, 1966, and 1970.

Most hat tricks – 92
Pelé had one eight-goal game, six five-goal games, and 30 four-goal games.

Pelé

Women's Game

Soccer is the most popular sport in the world for both men and women. Women have been playing soccer for hundreds of years. The first women's soccer leagues were started in the 1930s. In the 1970s and 1980s, women's soccer became popular in colleges and high schools. The U.S. national women's soccer team began playing in 1985. The success of this team helped the game grow in popularity. In 1996, the United States beat China for the Olympic gold medal. More than 76,000 people were in attendance at the game in Athens, Georgia, in the United States.

Tiffany Milbrett

HAMMER TIME

One of the greatest female soccer players of all time was a member of the 1996 U.S. Olympic team. Mia Hamm holds the record for most international goals. No man or woman has scored more international goals than Hamm, who has 158 goals for the U.S. She led her country to two Olympic gold medals, one silver, and two World Cup championships.

Groundbreakers

Soccer has been played for centuries. It began as a sport in Great Britain and spread to other parts of the world, such as Africa, the Caribbean, and South America. These countries have become known for

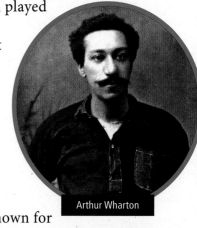
Arthur Wharton

their excellent soccer players. The first black soccer player to play for a national team was Andrew Watson in the 1870s. Watson was born in British Guiana and later moved to Scotland. He played for Queen's Park, as well as the Scottish national team. Watson was known as one of the best players in all of Great Britain.

Arthur Wharton was the first black **professional** soccer player. He was born in Ghana and moved to England in 1882. In 1886, Wharton signed his first professional contract as a goalkeeper with Preston North End.

Brazil has become known as one of the best soccer countries in the world. Many of the greatest Brazilian soccer players have been black. In 1914, Artur Friedenreich became the first black person to play for Brazil. Friedenreich played his entire career for Brazil and scored 1,329 goals. This is more than any other player from any country. With 1,281 goals, another Brazilian, Pelé, scored the second-highest number of goals.

The Keepers

Blue Streak

Italy is known for producing great soccer players and teams. The key to any successful soccer team is a skilled goalkeeper. Dino Zoff set two world records while playing for Italy. From September 1972 until June 1974, Zoff did not allow a single goal in international competition. After 1,142 minutes and almost 13 games of **clean sheet** soccer, Zoff let in a goal during a game against Haiti. In 1982, Zoff was Italy's captain, and he led his country to the World Cup championship. At 40 years old, Zoff was the oldest player ever to win the World Cup.

Dino Zoff

Goalie Goals

A goalkeeper's job is to keep balls out of the net. Sometimes, a goalkeeper helps the team in other ways, such as scoring goals. When a goalkeeper scores a goal, it is an amazing accomplishment because the nets are 270 feet (82 meters) apart. The record for most goals by a goalkeeper is held by Rogério Ceni, has played for Sao

Rogério Ceni

Paulo and Brazil. Ceni takes **free kicks** and **penalties** for Sao Paulo. He has scored 89 goals since 1997. If he misses a kick, Ceni must try to run back to his own net before the other team has a chance to score.

Filling the Net

William "Fatty" Foulke started playing for Sheffield United at 19 years old, replacing

William Foulke

Arthur Wharton in goal. Foulke was the largest goalkeeper in history. He stood 6 feet 3 inches (190.5 centimeters) tall and weighed more than 300 pounds (136 kg). Foulke was known to eat the entire team's breakfast and sit on people who made fun of his weight until they apologized. He once picked up a player on an opposing team and held him by his ankles over a muddy field. In 1907, Foulke wore a bed sheet because he was too large to fit a jersey. Foulke was very strong because of his large size. He once snapped the **crossbar** in two while making a save.

The Black Panther

Lev Yashin, who played for Dinamo Moscow in Russia from 1949 until 1971, is considered the greatest goalkeeper in soccer history. Yashin was called the Black Panther, the Black Spider, and the Black Octopus because of his black uniform and amazing speed and skill at blocking shots. Yashin played internationally for the **Soviet Union**, winning the 1956 Olympic gold medal and the 1960 European Championship. He also competed in three World Cups and won a Soviet ice hockey championship. Yashin is the only goalkeeper ever to win the **International Federation of Association Football** (FIFA) European Player of the Year award.

Lev Yashin

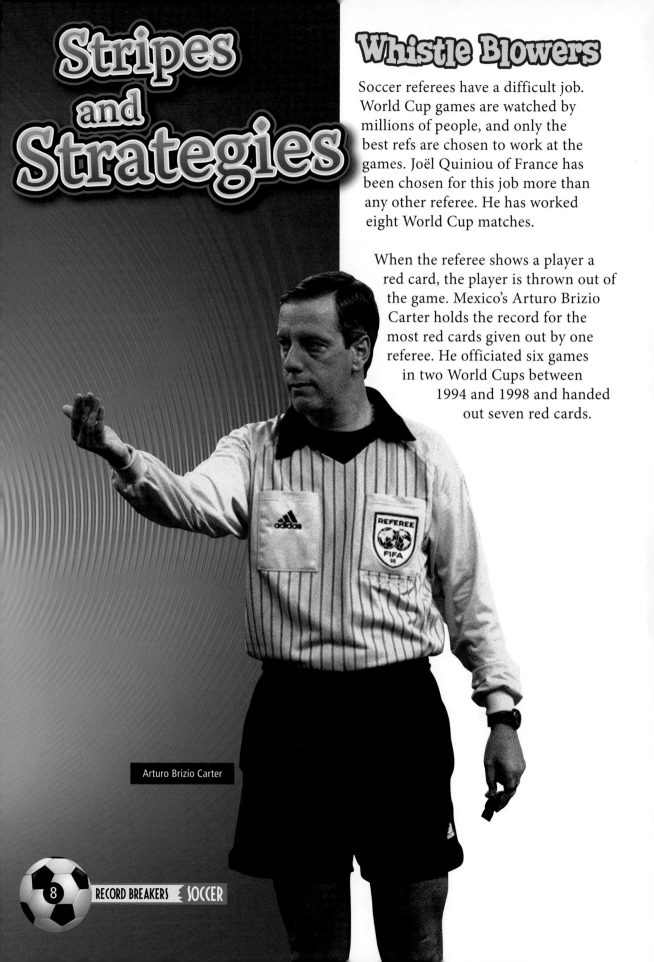

Stripes and Strategies

Whistle Blowers

Soccer referees have a difficult job. World Cup games are watched by millions of people, and only the best refs are chosen to work at the games. Joël Quiniou of France has been chosen for this job more than any other referee. He has worked eight World Cup matches.

When the referee shows a player a red card, the player is thrown out of the game. Mexico's Arturo Brizio Carter holds the record for the most red cards given out by one referee. He officiated six games in two World Cups between 1994 and 1998 and handed out seven red cards.

Arturo Brizio Carter

Leading the Charge

Here are some World Cup coaching records.

Bora Milutinovic
Most countries coached – 5

Mexico	1986
Costa Rica	1990
United States	1994
Nigeria	1998
China	2002

Vittorio Pozzo
Most championships – 2
1934, 1938

Helmut Schön
Most matches – 25
1966, 1970, 1974, 1978

Most wins – 16
1966, 1970, 1974, 1978

Masterful Management

One of the most successful soccer managers in history is Sir Alex Ferguson, who coaches Manchester United. Ferguson began his career as a player in the Scottish Premier League. He then began coaching in the same league. Ferguson became one of the top managers in the world while coaching Aberdeen. In 1986, he moved to Manchester and has since become a legend of the game. In his 24 years with Manchester United, Ferguson has led the team to 11 league titles, five Football Association (FA) Cups, and two Champions League trophies. In total, he has won more than 30 trophies in his time at Manchester.

Sir Alex Ferguson

9

The World Cup

Sizing It Up

The FIFA World Cup is the best-known soccer tournament in the world. Aside from the Olympics, it is the most watched sporting event. It attracts billions of television viewers. The World Cup trophy was designed in 1974 by Silvio Gazzaniga of Italy. It shows two players celebrating victory, holding the world over their heads. Each winning team keeps the trophy until the next World Cup. The solid gold trophy stands 12.6 inches (36 cm) high and weighs 13.6 pounds (6.2 kg). The bottom of the trophy is engraved with the name and year of each winning team since 1974.

Women's World

Women had their chance to be world champions 61 years after the first men's World Cup. The first women's World Cup was held in China in 1991, with the United States winning the title. There have been five women's World Cups, and the competition has grown in popularity with each event.

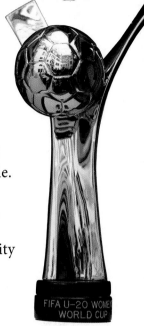

FIFA U-20 WOMEN WORLD CUP

Winner	Runner-Up	Host	Year
Germany	Brazil	China	2007
Germany	Sweden	United States	2003
United States	China	United States	1999
Norway	United States	Sweden	1995
United States	Norway	China	1991

Crown Jules

The World Cup trophy used today is not the original. The first World Cup was played in 1930 in Uruguay. The event was planned by Jules Rimet, the president of FIFA. Uruguay won the tournament, and the team was awarded the Jules Rimet Cup. This gold-plated, **sterling** silver statue stands 13.8 inches (35 cm) high and weighs 8.4-pound (3.8 kg). During World War II, the Jules Rimet Cup was hidden in a shoebox under the FIFA vice president's bed. In 1966, the cup was stolen. It was found by a dog named Pickles. The trophy had been buried under a tree in England. The cup was retired in 1970. It was given to Brazil, which had won the cup a record three times. The cup was stolen from Rio de Janeiro in 1983, and some people believe the thieves may have melted it for the gold.

★ CUP COLLECTORS ★

There have been 18 men's World Cup competitions since 1930. The home team has won six times. Home team winners include Uruguay in 1930, Italy in 1934, England in 1966, West Germany in 1974, Argentina in 1978, and France in 1998. In total, only seven countries have won the tournament, with Brazil winning the most.

Country	Championships	Year(s)
Brazil	5	1958, 1962, 1970, 1994, 2002
Italy	4	1934, 1938, 1982, 2006
West Germany	3	1954, 1974, 1990
Uruguay	2	1930, 1950
Argentina	2	1978, 1986
England	1	1966
France	1	1998

The Gear

The Pigskin

Soccer has been played since the **Middle Ages**. Today, soccer balls are high-tech pieces of equipment that are designed to fly through the air at fast speeds. Players kick the ball in different ways to make it spin, rise, or drop in midair. Hundreds of years ago, soccer balls were made from a pig's **bladder** that was filled with air. Later, balls were made from leather, with rubber interiors to hold the air. For the 1970 World Cup, 32 black and white panels were hand-stitched to create a rounder shape for the ball. The black and white panels made the ball easier to see on black and white television. Today, most soccer balls are made from **synthetic** materials.

Spikes

Many of the best soccer players in the world have their own **merchandise**. One of the most common types of soccer merchandise is shoes, or spikes. Ronaldinho, who plays for AC Milan in the Italian Série A, as well as Brazil, has a shoe deal with Nike. This deal, along with Ronaldinho's other **endorsement** deals, are worth $30 million a year.

Out of This Galaxy

David Beckham, the best-known soccer player in the world, announced that he had signed a contract with the Los Angeles Galaxy on July 11, 2007. It was the biggest deal in the history of soccer. By the time Beckham was introduced to fans only two days later, the team had already sold more than 250,000 jerseys printed with Beckham's name and number.

David Beckham

Jerseys

Soccer jerseys are used to tell teams and players apart on the field. Goalkeepers wear a different colored jersey than the other players on the team. This is so the referee can easily spot the goalkeeper. Players have their name and number on the back of the jersey and the team logo on the front. Most professional teams also have their sponsor's logo on the front of their jersey. Sponsors pay large amounts of money to have their logo on a team's jersey. Manchester United's sponsor, Aon Insurance, paid more than $120 million to have their logo on the jersey. The logo will first appear in the 2010 to 2011 season.

Alberto Aquilani

13

More Records

Young Guns

Soccer is a game that requires speed and **endurance**. Having both of these skills can give young players an advantage over older players. Players who start playing professionally at a young age often have long, successful careers. Here are the youngest players ever in the World Cup.

Player	Professional Start	Team	Year
Pelé	17 years, 249 days	Brazil	1958
Guiseppe Bergomi	18 years, 201 days	Italy	1982
Ruben Moran	19 years, 344 days	Uruguay	1950

Top Scorers

In international soccer, the World Cup is the most important tournament. The Union of European Football Associations (UEFA) Champions League tournament is the most important event for football teams in Europe. It takes a skilled team to earn a spot in each of these tournaments. Scoring goals is one of the most valuable skills in soccer. The players listed below have scored more goals in the World Cup and Champions League than any other players.

Most Goals in a single World Cup – 15
Ronaldo, Brazil

Most Career Goals in the Champions League – 66
Raúl, Real Madrid

Ronaldo

The Best of the Best

The Champions League is a competition between the best teams in Europe. The top teams from each league in Europe compete each year to determine a champion. Real Madrid has dominated the tournament since it began in 1956. Here are the teams that have won the most championships throughout the history of the event.

Team	Country	Championships	Years
Real Madrid	Spain	9	1956 to 1960, 1966, 1998, 2000, 2002
AC Milan	Italy	7	1963, 1969, 1989, 1990, 1994, 2003, 2007
Liverpool	England	5	1977, 1978, 1981, 1984, 2005
Ajax	Netherlands	4	1971 to 1973, 1995
Bayern Munich	Germany	4	1974 to 1976, 2001

On the Spot

Some people have broken soccer records without even playing in a game. Ball control is a skill that helps on the field. Juggling is a form of ball control. It is the act of keeping the ball in the air using only the feet, knees, shoulders, and head. These people have made it into the record books by having excellent ball control skills.

Longest time juggling – 24.5 hours
Nikolai Kutsenko, Ukraine

Speed juggling (male) – 185 touches in 30 seconds
John Stayskal, United States

Speed juggling (female) – 163 touches in 30 seconds
Chloe Hegland, Canada

Soccer Players Around the World

Soccer is a popular sport around the world. This map shows the goals that each player has scored for his country in international competition. These are the top scorers from each of these countries.

NORTH AMERICA

SOUTH AMERICA

United States

Landon Donovan

International Goals: 42

Brazil

Pelé

International Goals: 77

Argentina

Gabriel Batistuta

International Goals: 56

England

Bobby Charlton
International Goals: 49

ASIA

Portugal

Pauleta
International Goals: 47

EUROPE

AFRICA

Ivory Coast

Didier Drogba
International Goals: 43

AUSTRALIA

N
W E
S

621 Miles
0   1,000 Kilometers

17

The Pitch

The Theatre of Dreams

Old Trafford, the home stadium of Manchester United, is not the biggest or most beautiful stadium in the world, but it is full of history and legend. The stadium first became the home of Manchester United in 1910. In 1941, during World War II, the building was bombed by Germany. It took eight years to rebuild. The stadium seats more than 76,000 fans and has a museum that covers three floors.

The Original

Soccer is a sport full of history and tradition. Many teams still play on the same grounds they did more than 100 years ago.

The oldest soccer stadium is Sandygate Road in Crosspool, a suburb of Sheffield, England. The stadium opened in 1804, and Hallam FC have played there since 1860. The first **interclub** soccer match in the world took place at Sandygate Road when Hallam FC played the world's first soccer club, Sheffield FC.

Pelé receiving a membership to Sheffield FC

The Biggest Stadiums

Rungrado May Day Stadium in North Korea
Team: North Korean national team
Seats: 150,000

Salt Lake Stadium in Calcutta, India
Teams: Indian national team,
Mohun Bagan, East Bengal
Seats: 120,000 seats

Estadio Azteca in Mexico City, Mexico
Teams: Mexican national team, Club America
Seats: 105,000

Melbourne Cricket Ground in Melbourne, Australia
Team: Australian national team (Socceroos)
Seats: 100,000

Azadi Stadium in Tehran, Iran
Teams: Iranian national team, Perespolis FC, Esteghlal FC
Seats: 100,000

**Bukit Jalil National Stadium in Bukit Jalil,
Kuala Lumpur, Malaysia**
Team: Malaysian national team
Seats: 100,000

Costly Construction

In 2000, Wembley Stadium, the home of the national soccer team in England, was torn down. A new stadium was built in its place. The new Wembley stadium is the most expensive stadium ever built, costing more than $1.5 billion. It seats 90,000 fans and will host the soccer tournament of the 2012 Olympics.

In The Money

$ BIG BUSINESS $

Soccer teams are businesses. People pay huge amounts of money to own soccer teams. These are the most valuable soccer teams.

Manchester United, England – $1.9 billion

Real Madrid, Spain – $1.4 billion

Arsenal, England – $1.2 billion

Bayern Munich, Germany – $1.1 billion

Liverpool, England – $1 billion

Sporting Salaries

Soccer clubs pay large amounts of money to have the best players in the world on their team. Here are the top paid players in soccer.

Cristiano Ronaldo, Real Madrid
$16.2 million

Zlatan Ibrahimovic, FC Barcelona
$14.9 million

Lionel Messi, FC Barcelona
$13 million

Samuel Eto'o, Internazionale
$13 million

Kaká, Real Madrid
$12.4 million

Funding the Game

On average, how much do people spend at a soccer game?
Ticket: $25
Hot dog: $3.50
Soft drink: $3.50
Program: $5
Hat: $15

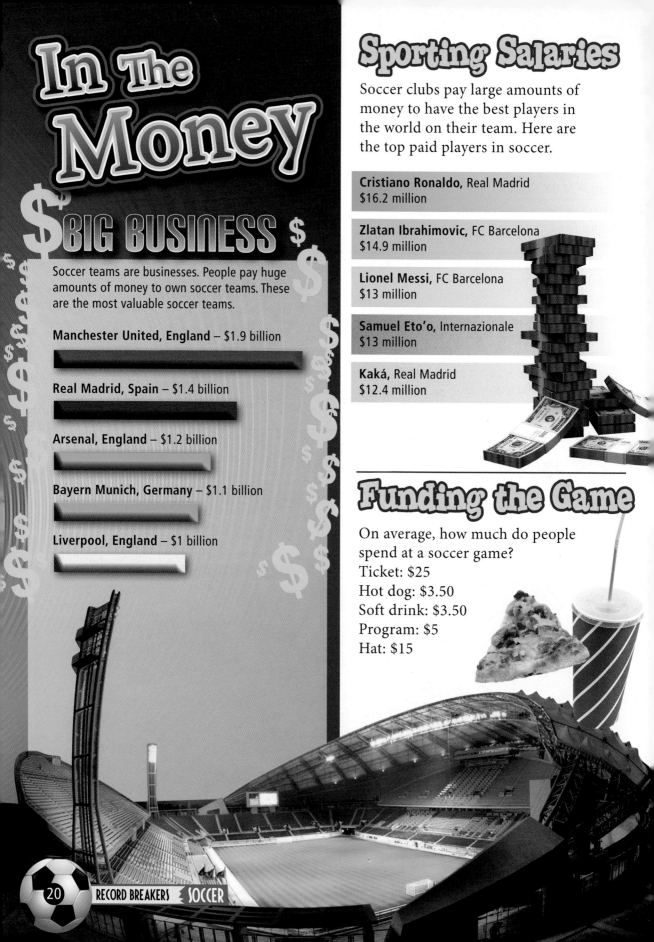

Culture

Sing Along

Soccer fans are known for being loud, energetic, and dedicated supporters of their teams. Many teams have songs or anthems that their fans sing during games. The best-known soccer song is "You'll Never Walk Alone," which is often sung by fans of Liverpool FC in England. The song was originally written in 1945 for a musical play called *Carousel*. It has been recorded by artists such as Frank Sinatra. Fans of other teams, including Celtic and Hibernian in Scotland, and Feyenoord in Holland, also sing this song.

Fan Mile

The World Cup is much more than just a soccer tournament. At the 2006 World Cup in Germany, about 500,000 people gathered each day in Berlin to watch soccer matches on huge screens that had been set up near the gates of the former Berlin Wall. People from all over the world came together at "Fan Fest" to watch games, listen to music, and look at the many displays of German culture. There was even a nightly laser show, huge sand sculptures, and soccer and volleyball game areas.

Bad Boys

Most soccer fans are well behaved, but occasionally, some fans behave poorly. Known as hooligans, these poor sports start fights and **riots**. In 1985, 39 Juventus fans were killed when a wall collapsed during a riot. Increasing security and creating stricter rules are a few of the ways soccer teams around the world are hoping to stop hooligans.

QUIZ

1 Who was the first black person to play professional soccer?

2 What are two of Lev Yashin's nicknames?

3 Who was the largest goalkeeper in history?

4 What country won the Jules Rimet Trophy three times?

5 What team has won the most Champions League tournaments?

6 Who has scored the most goals in history?

7 What is the most valuable soccer team?

8 How much did it cost to build the new Wembley Stadium?

9 Who is the highest-paid soccer player?

10 What is the name of the song sung by Liverpool fans?

ANSWERS: 1. Arthur Wharton 2. The Black Panther, Black Spider, and Black Octopus 3. William "Fatty" Foulke 4. Brazil 5. Real Madrid 6. Artur Friedenreich 7. Manchester United 8. more than $1.5 billion 9. David Beckham 10. "You'll Never Walk Alone"

GLOSSARY

bladder: an organ inside the body that collects and disposes of urine

cease-fire: an agreement between two groups to stop fighting

clean sheet: not allowing any goals in a game

crossbar: the horizontal beam that makes the top part of the net

endorsement: a deal in which a player agrees to help sell a product

endurance: having enough energy to perform an act for a long period of time

free kicks: the act of allowing a player to kick the ball without pressure from the other team

Hebrew: Jewish language and culture

interclub: a game between two clubs

International Federation of Association Football (FIFA): the organization that rules over international soccer competition

merchandise: items that are bought and sold

Middle Ages: a period in history between the years 1100 and 1453

penalties: free kicks from a place on the field that is in front of the goal; the goalkeeper must defend the net without the help of other team members

professional: a player who is paid to play

riots: violent acts by a crowd of people

Soviet Union: a former group of countries in Eastern Europe with Moscow as the capital; relating to the U.S.S.R.

sterling: high-quality silver

synthetic: a humanmade product that is similar to a product found in nature

INDEX

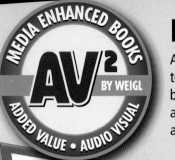

Log on to www.av2books.com

AV² by Weigl brings you media enhanced books that support active learning. Go to **www.av2books.com**, and enter the special code inside the front cover of this book. You will gain access to enriched and enhanced content that supplements and complements this book. Content includes video, audio, web links, quizzes, a slide show, and activities.

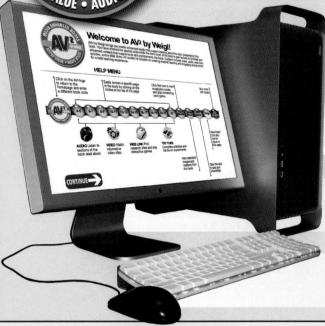

Audio
Listen to sections of the book read aloud.

Video
Watch informative video clips.

Web Link
Find research sites and play interactive games.

Try This!
Complete activities and hands-on experiments.

WHAT'S ONLINE?

Try This! Complete activities and hands-on experiments.	Web Link Find research sites and play interactive games.	Video Watch informative video clips.	EXTRA FEATURE
Pages 10-11 Try this soccer activity.	**Pages 6-7** Learn more about soccer goalkeepers.	**Pages 4-5** Watch a video about soccer.	**Audio** Hear introductory at the top of every
Pages 12-13 Test your knowledge of soccer gear.	**Pages 8-9** Read about coaches, managers, and referees.	**Pages 14-15** View stars of the sport in action.	**Key Words** Study vocabulary, and play a matching word game.
Pages 16-17 Complete this mapping activity.	**Pages 18-19** Find out more about where soccer games take place.	**Pages 20-21** Watch a video about soccer players.	**Slide Show** View images and captions, and try a writing activity.
			AV² Quiz Take this quiz to test your knowledge

Due to the dynamic nature of the Internet, some of the URLs and activities provided as part of AV² by Weigl may have changed or ceased to exist. AV² by Weigl accepts no responsibility for any such changes. All media enhanced books are regularly monitored to update addresses and sites in a timely manner. Contact AV² by Weigl at 1-866-649-3445 or av2books@weigl.com with any questions, comments, or feedback.